HERMAN VANDENBURG AMES

Herman V. Ames

Memorial

HERMAN VANDENBURG AMES

Late Professor of American Constitutional History University of Pennsylvania

Edited by

EDWARD P. CHEYNEY

AND

ROY F. NICHOLS

University of Pennsylvania Press
PHILADELPHIA
1936

Manufactured in the United States of America

London
Humphrey Milford
Oxford University Press

HERMAN VANDENBURG AMES

Foreword

THE WINTER of 1934-35 was bitter even in Philadelphia, and the evening of February 6 was particularly inclement. Nevertheless Dr. Ames, as one of the representatives of the American Philosophical Society, went then on an important mission to a distant country house. Late that night he was stricken without warning, and within a few hours died as peacefully as he had lived. He had been spared the wearying years of decline and to the last was fully active in his many interests.

On May 7, 1935, a memorial meeting was held in Houston Auditorium at the University of Pennsylvania where many gathered to pay final tribute. The words then spoken are here recorded, accompanied by a few of the many letters and memorials written in appreciation of Dr. Ames's long life of service to education and scholarship. Miss Ames and the members of the History Department of the University of Pennsylvania unite in presenting this memorial to his friends.

HERMAN VANDENBURG AMES

Contents

Dr. Ames was born August 7, 1865, at Lancaster, Massachusetts, son of Rev. Marcus and Jane Vandenburg Ames. He died February 7, 1935, at Philadelphia.

HERMAN VANDENBURG AMES

Memorial Addresses

A MEMORIAL meeting for Dr. Ames was held in Houston Hall of the University of Pennsylvania, May 7, 1935. Some three hundred persons were present. Professor Edward P. Cheyney, his oldest living colleague in the Department of History, in introducing the speakers made the remarks which follow.

We have come to honor the memory of Dr. Herman V. Ames, to express our appreciation of his character and services and in some degree our affection for him. A few weeks have intervened since his death, scarcely enough time to allow us to overcome our shock and incredulity, and to weigh and measure our sense of loss. Others will speak of him from their respective points of view. It is my part only to give a somewhat personal setting to what may be said. This I have a right to do, for we have met almost daily through a large part of each year for almost forty years; and I think I can fairly represent not only our personal relations but those of our small group of members of the History Department. It was, I think, a matter of surprise to all of us to learn, or at least to realize, that he was in his seventieth year. He had changed so little through the years, his temperament was so even, his interests so responsive, that the passing years touched him lightly and made him seem, to me at least, the same man of early middle life who had come to the University in 1897.

His ancestry was reflected in his character. His father, Rev. Marcus Ames, was an active reformer during most of the years of his life. He was head of a school for delinquent girls at Lancaster, Mass., one of the first in the country, and chaplain of the various penal institutions of Rhode Island. Dr. Ames thus inherited an interest in social welfare and public service which made deep impress upon his life. His evenness of temper, tolerant spirit, and integrity may well have been an inheritance from the Vandenburgs, his Dutch forebears on his mother's side; no one could fail to recognize him at the same time as a New Englander, coming down in more than one line and drawing more than one characteristic from the group who came over in the Mayflower. To those of us who are not Presbyterians he did not seem to fill the part of elder in a Presbyterian congregation, as we imagine it, but such he was. If a man must go through life unmarried, as he did, he was fortunate in having a sister to whose devotion and sympathetic companionship we can all testify.

His was a typical academic career. He studied in five colleges and universities in this country and abroad, and taught in six. He was loyal to them all. If he sometimes seemed to show a specially warm feeling for Amherst, that is no more than is generally true of the college in which one spends his most plastic years, and no more than Amherst seems generally fortunate in receiving from her sons. Certainly from 1897 forward he was a genuine and a devoted Pennsylvania man. He enjoyed and suffered from all the implications of an academic career; many classes, graduate and undergraduate, many committee memberships, long service in one of the most important administrative positions, the constant struggle to find time to renew one's contact with the sources of knowledge in one's special field and even to contribute to its advance. No one can testify to this side of the career of Dr. Ames more suitably than Provost Penniman.

DR. PENNIMAN

Ladies and Gentlemen, Friends, Colleagues, and Students of Dr. Ames:

We have paused this afternoon for a short time to pay a tribute of respect, appreciation, and affection to the memory of Herman Vandenburg Ames, who for more than the average length of a generation of men was an Instructor and Professor in the Department of American History at this University (1897-1935), and for twenty-one years (from 1907 to 1928) the honored Dean of the Graduate School of Arts and Science. Before coming to the University of Pennsylvania, Dr. Ames, a graduate of Amherst 1888, and a graduate student at Columbia and Harvard, from the latter of which he received his Ph.D. degree in 1891, taught at the University of Michigan from 1891 to 1894, studied at Leipzig and Heidelberg 1894-95, and taught at Ohio State University 1896-97. The University of Pennsylvania conferred upon him the honorary degree of Doctor of Letters in 1925, and La Salle College, Philadelphia, conferred upon him the degree of Doctor of Laws in 1927.

Dr. Ames was editor of *State Documents on Federal Relations: The States and the United States.* He was the author of *Proposed Amendments to the Constitution of the United*

States (awarded in 1897, the Justin Winsor prize of the American Historical Association); *Outline of Lectures on American Political and Institutional History during the Colonial and Revolutionary Periods*, 3d edition, 1908; *Syllabus of American Colonial History* (with Dr. W. T. Root), 1912.

Dr. Ames taught American History at the Columbia summer sessions, 1906-7, University of Wisconsin summer session, 1908, University of California summer session, 1927. He was Chairman of the Archives Commission, 1902-12, and Member of the Council, 1911-14, of the American Historical Association; Secretary, 1900-3, and Member of the Executive Committee, 1903-5, of the Association of Colleges and Preparatory Schools of the Middle States and Maryland; Member of the National Conference Commission on Standards of Colleges and Secondary Schools, 1906-13; President of the Middle States Association of History Teachers, 1909-10; Member of the Executive Committee, 1918-22, and Chairman of Committee on International Educational Relations, 1919-24, of the American Council on Education; Member of the Administrative Board, Institute of International Education, since 1919.

In addition to his work as a teacher and administrator, Dr. Ames was active in a number of organizations, being a member of the Pennsylvania War History Commission 1918-21. He was Governor-General, Order of Founders and Patriots of America 1919-21, Deputy Governor General Society Mayflower Descendants since 1930; Member of American Philosophical Society; American Political Science Association; American Antiquarian Society; Historical Society of Pennsylvania, (Member of Council 1926-35); Philadelphia Geographical Society (member of Council 1927-30); University Club.

Dr. Ames was prominent in the Presbyterian Church, of which he was a lifelong member, and was an elder in the Second Church of Philadelphia. Although I have been closely associated with Dr. Ames during the entire period of his service at the University of Pennsylvania, it is as Dean of the Graduate School that I knew him best. I know of no dean who was more deeply interested in the graduate students of the University, not only those who were studying American History, but all who were studying in any courses. The work of investigation had especial appeal to Dr. Ames, and his innumerable conferences with students who sought his advice and friendship mark his administration as characterized notably by his personal relations to the student body. He had a keen sense of humor, a deep sense of responsibility for the well-being of his students, a fine sympathy with them, and a kindly interest in all that concerned them. Throughout the length and breadth of the country are now men and women who received their training at the University of Pennsylvania during Dr. Ames's term as Dean. Without exception, their feeling for him continued after they had received their degrees and had taken up their individual labors. The scholarship of Dr. Ames was sound and broad, and he was highly respected by historians.

I like to think of Dr. Ames as being in his quiet way a great influence on the spiritual life of those who knew him, and in this connection may I quote to you, as applicable to him, two statements, one about George Eliot, and the other by Matthew Arnold, in setting forth his philosophy. George Eliot and

Matthew Arnold were both great ethical teachers; each of them left an indelible imprint upon contemporary thought.

George Eliot made a great contribution to the thought of her generation and moved men's minds singularly by her teaching that neither scorn nor laughter is so powerful as sympathy in human relations. *Romola*, *Middlemarch* and *Daniel Deronda* are all thoughtful arraignments of the criticism and cynicism of her forerunners.

Matthew Arnold wrote:

He who works for sweetness and light works to make reason and the will of God prevail. Culture has one great passion, the passion for sweetness and light. It has one even greater! the passion for making them *prevail*.

THE CHAIRMAN

Dr. Ames was more often spoken of by his colleagues, the students, and even outside of University circles as *Dean* Ames. This was the natural result of his long services as Dean of the Graduate School. Dean Crosby, his successor in that office, will speak of him in that capacity.

DR. CROSBY

It is manifestly fitting that in paying tribute to the memory of Herman V. Ames reference should be made to his distinguished career as Dean of the Graduate School of Arts and Science. I believe that I am correct in stating that when he resigned that post in February of 1928 he was the senior member of the Board of Deans, his term of service reaching back to the year 1907. So closely had he identified himself with graduate studies at the University of Pennsylvania that for most of us here, I am sure, the word "Dean" had become a permanent part of his name. At the present time, more than seven years after he surrendered to his successor both title and responsibilities, mail intended for the Graduate School still comes from all quarters of the globe addressed in his name.

When he first took up the deanship, most of the pioneering work in the organization of graduate studies at this university had already been performed under the able leadership of such men as Child and Newbold; Pennsylvania had already won recognition as a champion of the higher learning, both sane and inspiring; the Graduate School had a faculty of sixty-nine members, whose offering of courses covered forty-four printed pages; 316 men and women made up the student body.

To safeguard so fine a tradition of scholarly standards and achievement was no mean responsibility. How faithfully that responsibility was carried is only partially suggested by the observation that when Ames laid down his deanship in 1928 the Faculty had increased to two hundred and twenty-five, the courses offered covered one hundred and fourteen pages, and the student body numbered 1,560, not counting 457 that had attended graduate courses during the previous summer session.

The size of an institution is not a safe index of its stability and health. But those of his colleagues who were in the closest touch with Dean Ames, especially those who through the years were privileged to work with him on the Executive Committee, will testify to his intellectual integrity, to his unswerving devotion to the maintenance of high standards, to his valiant struggle to win for the Graduate School its rightful place in the economy of the University and to improve the conditions under which students and Faculty labored.

He suffered some disappointments. His Faculty did not always support him in reforms that he regarded of high importance, yet he bore no malice. He would have welcomed the establishment of a real budget for the Graduate School, affording the opportunity for leadership in the development of scholarship, but his spirit was such that he could lay aside that dream and by friendly collaboration with fellow deans and department heads build a school whose reputation spread far and wide, but over which he ruled largely by tolerance. It is no secret that Bennett Hall, toward whose erection he looked forward with such high hopes, when after long delay it finally took form, did not completely match his ideal vision of a home for graduate studies. That and other disappointments he accepted with a philosophic optimism that would not be discouraged and made the best of facilities provided.

It is indeed for these qualities of mind and heart—his patience, sincerity, idealism tempered by a clear-eyed realism, and his sympathetic understanding of human beings—that he will be remembered longest.

The conditions under which he labored for most of his deanship were conducive to the development of such qualities. Those of us who knew the university a quarter century ago recall that the office of the Graduate School was housed in a single room in College Hall. As you entered the door you faced across the room an old-fashioned roll-top desk surmounted by a row of thick volumes completely screening from observation the person of the Dean, but constituting in no sense a bar to the sound of his genial voice as he conversed in his friendly manner with student or colleague. He was easy of access, and most of us paid little heed to his office hours painted on the entrance.

A single clerk assisted in the varied duties of the office, and all the business was conducted within the hearing of the Dean, if not actually under his kindly eye. Of necessity he acquired an intimate knowledge of students and of their problems, and his retentive memory could be relied upon for pertinent details long after those students had gone far away. Not only was his interest in their welfare genuine, but they knew it and they came to look to him for friendly assistance.

That intimate acquaintance became less easy as the enrollment passed the thousand mark and the Graduate School moved into Bennett Hall. It must have been a source of real regret to the Dean that now he had a room all to himself. His personal interest had not diminished, but the satisfaction of that interest had become vastly more difficult and he chafed at the realization. He confessed the fear that he was growing irritable and offered that as a valid reason for his resignation. Few of us had seen signs to justify that fear.

That kindly human interest to which reference has just been made manifested itself in all his relations, both at home and abroad. He represented the University of Pennsylvania in connection with many associations and commissions, always with dignity. He was particularly active and valuable as our representative on the Association of American Universities, an association to which universities gain admission as members primarily because of the high standing of the graduate instruction that they maintain. Ames was an active member on many committees of that organization, and the respect for his sanity, alertness, integrity, and friendliness which he aroused in such relations was naturally and readily transferred to the institution that he represented. Pennsylvania enjoys a higher esteem in the eyes of sister universities because of the personal qualities he so consistently exhibited.

In closing this inadequate account, the speaker wishes to record his sense of personal indebtedness to Dean Ames for many deeds of kindness experienced through the years, but especially for his generous helpfulness and ready counsel in administering the office that he had relinquished. Never critical toward his successor nor officious in offering suggestions, Ames was ready at all times to come at call, unselfishly giving of his new-found leisure for the purpose of aiding the tyro and serving the University. And so I count it a high privilege to join in this tribute to his memory. May it ever remain green.

THE CHAIRMAN

Reference has been made by the Provost and in the sketches of the life of Dr. Ames that have been published in the newspapers to the many outside bodies with which he was connected; the American Historical Association, the Historical Society of Pennsylvania, the American Philosophical Society, the Mayflower Society, and other organizations. As representative of these Mr. Edward Robins, Vice President of the Historical Society of Pennsylvania, will speak of him and read a message from the Officers and Council of that Society.

MR. ROBINS

The President and Council of the Historical Society of Pennsylvania have asked me to express to those assembled here their profound regret at the death of Herman Vandenburg Ames. To do this, and to pay a brief but sincere tribute to his memory, is for me a sympathetic duty. For it was my privilege to know Dr. Ames more or less intimately during the time he was Dean of the Graduate School and Professor of American Constitutional History and I was Secretary of the University of Pennsylvania, and, later on, when he became one of our most distinguished associates on the Council of the Historical Society. In the latter capacity he was invaluable to us, for it is hardly necessary to say that he was, so to speak, steeped in the literature of American history. In addition he was very helpful in suggestions as to our administrative problems. Needless to add that we greatly admired him and often looked to him for inspiration.

Dr. Ames became a member of the Historical Society in October 1900, a Councillor from 1926 to 1930, and our Corresponding Secretary in the last-named year. He also served on various committees. Let me note, in a general way, that he gracefully filled the part which is indicated by the old-fashioned term "a gentleman and a scholar." To quote our minutes "He was both, and he possessed, besides, a keen common sense which made his advice so welcome to the Council. In his personal life he was friendly, genial, and unaffected, with a pleasant sense of humor, and although he won due reputation and honor as an historian (including the degrees of Doctor of Letters and Doctor of Laws) it all came to him without his seeking."

The Historical Society has lost a wise counselor and sterling friend, upon whose like we shall not look soon again. May we of the Historical Society offer to the University of Pennsylvania this imperfect but heartfelt record in memoriam.

THE CHAIRMAN

I suppose there is no college professor or other teacher who does not value, above all other rewards, such impress as he may have made on his students. It is there, if anywhere, our life-work may have been fruitful. We cannot, like artists or architects or engineers, leave visible and tangible results of our efforts, and our books are often but the by-products of our industry, written under difficult conditions, far below our ideals and destined to be soon superseded or forgotten. But we can always have faith, and often receive assurance that we have really influenced the lives of our students. It is in search of testimony on this point that Dr. Ames's colleagues have asked to attend this meeting, and to speak for his graduate students, one whose influential career since must have made him especially appreciative of what was done for him as a student. Dr. John Musser, Professor of History in New York University, will speak as representative, so far as any one man can represent so large and diverse a body, of Dr. Ames's students.

DR. MUSSER

It would be unbecoming and ungrateful for me not to appreciate the honor of this opportunity to pay tribute to the memory of my respected teacher and dear friend, Dr. Ames. My only fear is that I cannot adequately represent the large group of graduates on behalf of whom I am speaking, and who, I am sure, whether present in person or only in spirit, are sharing our sense of loss in the passing of the man whose character and services we are here commemorating. I can, however, plead that few if any of Dean Ames's students were in more intimate contact with him, and I am sure that to none did his death bring a more real sense of personal loss. For three years I was his assistant, and in two additional years I sat under him in at least two courses a year. Through the almost daily contacts over those five years there developed a personal friendship that rose superior to the usual relations of teacher and student.

Teacher in the University in the grades from instructor to professor for a period of thirty-seven years, Dean of the Graduate School for twenty-one years (almost half of its organized existence) Dr. Ames has left an indelible impress on the hosts of students who passed through his classrooms, and on the even larger number who came under his administrative oversight as Dean.

During the period in which Dr. Ames served as Dean of the Graduate School the University conferred the doctorate on almost seventy students in History, the majority of whom are now engaged in college or university teaching in institutions from Massachusetts to Georgia and North Carolina, from New York to California and Oregon, from Illinois and Wisconsin to Texas and Wyoming. Interested as he was during this period in the graduate students in all departments, yet he seemed to feel an especially close relationship to the young men and women who were working in his own loved field of History. It is this group in general that knew him best and owe him most. To us he was first administrator, then scholarly exemplar, revered teacher, and trusted friend.

Provost Penniman has spoken of his administrative relationship with the University. To the students who came to his office he was always easily accessible, uniformly courteous, and invariably anxious to help with their problems. His advice was sincere and frank, kindly but always honest. Maintaining the highest standards, without in any way being a mere stickler for rules or formalities, he could reprove in a way that tended to bring response in corrective efforts rather than to cause discouragement. No trouble was too great if it were to assist the deserving, but with the indolent and careless he had little patience and could be advisedly severe. I never have heard a student or graduate express a word of criticism as to his fairness or justice, in itself a tribute to his success as an administrator that any university executive officer might well envy.

To many of us it is a source of regret that Dr. Ames, because of the burden of his administrative and teaching duties, could not devote more of his scholarly and critical ability to research, but "of the making of many books there is no end," and he consciously, although undoubtedly at times with real regret, laid aside many of his own studies to serve the University and the cause of learning in other ways. Yet on numerous desks and shelves throughout the country there are copies of certain of his works, especially his *State Documents on Federal Relations* and the *Proposed Amendments to the Constitution of the United States*, their worn and battered condition mute evidence of continued usefulness.

The most lasting impressions of his teaching are those of his absolute and always conscientious thoroughness, his painstaking accuracy, his critical point of view, and above all his impartiality. Although born in Massachusetts, educated at Amherst and Harvard, Governor General of the Order of Founders and Patriots of America, Deputy Governor General of the Society of Mayflower Descendants, deservedly proud of his Pilgrim ancestry and of his New England background, he would have scorned the idea that such factors should influence his teaching or affect his viewpoint as a scholar. Neither in the field of Colonial History, nor in his courses on the Civil War and the Reconstruction Period was there any reflection of sectional or partisan views or influences. To him History served only the cause of truth. The idea now held by some scholars, even some of considerable repute, that the purposes of History are to create a philosophy of action, to establish material standards of values, to serve the ends of party, class, or national interest would have seemed to him intolerable heresy. Whatever an historian might be he was not to be a propagandist, and because complete objectivity and absolute impartiality are perhaps impossible to attain was no reason why the noble goal implied should be abandoned. I sometimes think he himself possessed the judicial mind to an eminent degree, and if he had selected the law as a life career that he would have made a great jurist.

To many of the alumni Dr. Ames was not only respected administrator and teacher, but a loved friend who took a personal interest in their social organizations, their problems, their ambitions, and their hopes. While at the University they found hospitable welcome in his home, a welcome which was extended by his sister as well as himself, and when they left he took pains to keep in touch with their careers, and felt pride in their achievements.

I feel however that "I tell that which you yourselves do know" that Pennsylvania, the University he loved so well, in honoring Dean Ames honors herself. For myself and for the host of the alumni that I represent I can only say, "He was my friend, faithful and just to me."

THE CHAIRMAN

In closing this memorial meeting may I speak a few words personally of the place Dr. Ames held as a member of our small group, the History Department. Dr. Ames's interest in music, and his habit of travel, was in a certain sense a possession of all of us. Sometimes in the constant tendency to specialization, it is a little hard to keep up with an interest in one another's scholarly work, and there is even in the practical work of the department some discord. But in music, in art, in general literature, in the wide world of travel, there is always an opportunity for the comparison of interest and experiences—a wider and sometimes a less contentious atmosphere. Then, Dr. Ames had the happy faculty of seeming at leisure. In the midst of the hurried life we are so apt to lead and the restlessness we are so apt to betray, the man who can seem and really be, notwithstanding his many hours of teaching and administrative work, always calm and composed is an invaluable example and support.

Finally, there was a characteristic of Dr. Ames that I find it hard to name or describe, but which was none the less real, a certain dignity without any suggestion of pomposity, a certain urbanity, which was perhaps nothing more than genuine good manners, but which seemed to me admirable and, in our perhaps too informal manners, unusual. More than once I have thought during the last few weeks, as applicable to Dr. Ames both in his life and in his death, the ascription of the philosophic poet.

> So live, that when thy summons comes to join
> The innumerable caravan which moves
> To that mysterious realm where each shall take
> His chamber in the silent halls of death,
> Thou go not, like the quarry-slave at night,
> Scourged to his dungeon, but sustained and soothed
> By an unfaltering trust, approach thy grave
> Like one that wraps the drapery of his couch
> About him, and lies down to pleasant dreams.

HERMAN VANDENBURG AMES

Letters and Resolutions

DR. ALBERT BUSHNELL HART

I HELD him in great esteem as one of a group of graduate students who went out from Harvard to organize and put in action a scientific method of teaching history and government.

He had a host of friends and I never heard of his having a single enemy. His personal bearing . . . was always friendly, gracious and interested. We all know how much he did to make American history, and especially American government, a study on scientific grounds, not merely institutions but the character of great men, the development of governmental organization, the spirit of American organization and progress.

Personally I was much attached to Dr. Ames—we were fast friends as pupil and teacher and then as co-workers in the development of new men to carry on the work.

Personally and professionally I deeply deplore the end of his life career—but it is not ended. He has sowed the seed of search for truth in hundreds of minds. His work lives after him.

DR. JOHN FRAZER

Dr. Ames possessed to a remarkable degree those qualities of heart and mind which characterize the real scholar and which always endeared him to his colleagues who respected his integrity, his ability and his great modesty.

It was my good fortune to serve with him for a period of sixteen years on the Board of Deans during which time I always had the greatest respect and admiration for him.

The Graduate School, under his able administration, requiring much tact, patience and forbearance, enjoyed a remarkable development during the twenty odd years in which he guided its destinies and while ably carrying out this work, he found time for activities in numerous other fields.

DR. WINFRED T. ROOT

I owe a great deal to him: more than I can say. All through my graduate course it was a real pleasure to work under him as my major professor. In class room, in seminar, in personal conferences, he was always kindly and patient, generous of his time, and a fine scholar in the direction of my work.

It was under his direction and scholarly criticism my thesis saw its way to completion. Through his kindly offices I found a place to publish my thesis. It was through his influence I found a position.

EZRA POUND, COLLEGE '05

Rapallo, Italy, April 8, 1935

I am very sorry to hear of Dr. Ames' death, and there is an added drop of regret that he shouldn't have had the minor entertainment of knowing that his patiences and indulgences of 30 years ago hadn't been wholly wasted on one of his most cantankerous pupils.

I don't remember how long he had been teaching in 1901, 1902, and there may be students with longer memories but this note and the one that missed him, at least prove over and above any mere opinion that his courses had a vitality outlasting the mere time of his lectures. After thirty years, I still have pleasant recollection of "Reconstruction" and "Foreign Relations" courses, part and parcel of the recollection of the abundant and mellow good humour that pervaded his every act. "Gravity," says Sterne, "a mysterious carriage of the body to conceal the defects of the mind." No man in the University maintained a superior serenity or was freer from heaviness.

The ability to see things in proportion is certainly the historian's stronghold. To be undisturbed and undistracted by ping pong balls (the game was new at the beginning of this century, and the history room was furnished with long if narrow tables) or by the six foot two of Jimmy Kirkbride, looking longer on the flat one day when he fell over my shin-bone (with assistance) thus obstructing the free passage of Prof. Ames from his office into the class room, was characteristic of him. Such details as I recall, never obtruded themselves unduly into Dr. Ames' perspective. He did not make mountains out of molehills. The idea that a student might have a legitimate curiosity was in no way alien to his [Dr. Ames'] sensibilities. All of which goes into the making of a strong personal affection lasting over three decades with no more nutriment than perhaps two or three letters.

That a professor should as man leave this memory of respect and affection, and, as teacher, a still living interest in the subject he presented to one, as adolescent, is, I think, full measure of the good life, and proof of humanity overcoming all systems and invented partitions. Have we any better epitaph than old chief's: "The crops will be thick in my death year."

FROM RESOLUTIONS ADOPTED BY THE COLLEGE FACULTY

He represented the University of Pennsylvania with distinction on many committees and boards. In consequence of his multitudinous duties his writings were not as numerous as might otherwise have been the case. He had a high regard for scholarship and the product of his pen attests his capacity for scholarly accomplishment.

But it is rather in the domain of human relationships that he will be long remembered. Kindly and sympathetic toward students and colleagues, genial yet dignified, tolerant of the opinions of others yet unswerving in matters of principle, modest regarding his own attainments yet proud of the institution that he served so long and faithfully, he has left a record that will be cherished by alumni and fellow workers.

MEMORIAL READ AT THE ANNUAL MEETING OF THE AMERICAN HISTORICAL ASSOCIATION, 1935

Herman Vandenburg Ames, who died on February 7, 1935, for many of the years of his long career played a dual role as historian and educational administrator. He was active simultaneously as Professor of American Constitutional History and as Dean of the Graduate School at the University of Pennsylvania.

In the field of scholarship he devoted himself to the study of constitutional procedure and to the promotion of research. His monograph *Proposed Amendments to the Constitution* received the first Justin Winsor prize awarded by this Association. He explored the field of federal and state relations and published a volume of significant documents with appropriate introductory material. He promoted research in a seminar which he conducted for several decades. When the Association undertook the work of surveying and preserving the archives of all the states in the Union in 1899 he became interested at once and took the lead in the work for the Commonwealth of Pennsylvania. From 1902 to 1912 he directed the nationwide survey as chairman of the Association's Public Archives Commission, and superintended the publication of its extensive reports which have proved valuable tools for research workers. From 1911 to 1914 he served on the Association's council.

Educational administration, however, made ever greater demands upon him. In 1907 he became Dean of the Graduate School at the University of Pennsylvania, and he filled this rather trying post with wisdom, dignity, and organizing ability. During these years he continued an active teaching schedule and a vigorous interest in the generations of graduate students who passed through his office and seminar. To these students he was devoted; time was never too valuable to spare to them and no problem too trivial to receive his sympathetic counsel. Among his colleagues he was ever even-tempered, congenial, and considerate. He combined administrative talent with genuine sincerity, a combination too rare in the educational world.

Dr. Ames was a member of this organization for forty-five

of its fifty years of existence, and in pausing to honor his memory the American Historical Association pays tribute to one of the group who in the formative years joined in setting for it a high standard of excellence.

HERMAN VANDENBURG AMES

A Fragment of Autobiography Sent to an Amherst Reunion

DEAR CLASSMATES:

I am, indeed, pleased to hear that it is proposed that '88 should publish an autobiographical record of each of our surviving members. Not only will it be of deep interest to each of us, but also, I feel that we owe it to ourselves and to the College to place on record "the modest story" of our activities, as we have published nothing of the kind for thirty years.

My own lot has fallen in pleasant places. Graduation did not end my "college days," for either as student or teacher, and generally as both, the entire period since has been spent in academic life. For three years after leaving Amherst I pursued graduate work, for one year at Columbia, and the next two years at Harvard (A.M. 1890; Ph.D. 1891). Then for three years I attempted the job of teaching various periods of history from the Dawn of Civilization to Modern Times at the University of Michigan. I had specialized in American History, so that I was not particularly prepared for my task, but one must make a beginning somewhere, and this was the opening offered. The experience was a valuable one to me, far more so, I fear, than to the students taught. I formed many warm and enduring friendships, and I was afforded the opportunity to become acquainted with the life and work of the leading State University of the time, then under the direction of that "grand old man," President Angell, who was distinguished both as an educator and diplomatist.

Feeling the need of first-hand knowledge of European countries and in particular of German university methods, I spent fifteen months in Europe, attending lectures in history for a semester each at the universities of Leipsic and Heidelberg. I also made "the grand tour," as well as several "detours" into less frequented paths. My experiences and observations, while not having any immediate bearing on the subject of American Constitutional History, which I was destined to teach during the subsequent years, proved to be of decided value—not only by reason of the cultural influences afforded, but also due to the acquisition of a knowledge of European educational institutions and methods. The latter was to be of decided practical use in my later work as Dean and in my international educational contacts.

I returned from Europe too late in the summer to secure a teaching position. This proved to be a blessing in disguise as I was led to devote the year 1895-96 to research and to the revision of my doctor's thesis. The latter won the prize (The Justin Winsor) given by the American Historical Association, then awarded for the first time, but what was more important, it seems to have been responsible a year later, when published, for my invitation to teach at the University of Pennsylvania. In the meantime, I filled a temporary position at the Ohio State

University at Columbus, teaching both European and American History. In the fall of 1897, I entered upon my work at Pennsylvania where I am completing thirty-one years of service in charge of the work in American Constitutional History in both the graduate and undergraduate schools of the University. In addition, for the past twenty and more years (1907-28) I have been Dean of the Graduate School of Arts and Science. In February of the present year I retired from the position as Dean in order to devote my time wholly to my professorship. During my period of service as Dean, the Graduate School grew from an enrollment of some three hundred to upwards of sixteen hundred students, and the Faculty from about sixty-one to over 225 members.

Through my position as Dean I was brought in contact with various educational associations, especially the Association of American Universities, consisting of the Graduate Schools of the leading universities of this country and Canada, and the American Council on Education. For five years I have served as Secretary of the former, and as Chairman of the Committee on Educational Relations of the latter body from its establishment in 1918 until its recent merger with The American University Union into the International Institute of Education, of which latter body I have been a director for several years. Through these associations I have become much interested in the consideration of various problems connected with higher education both in this and other countries.

In the historical field, I have been an officer in various general and local historical societies. For ten years I served as Chairman of the Public Archives Commission of the American

Historical Association, and edited its annual reports, which related chiefly to the State Archives of this country. In addition, I am a member of the Councils of the American Philosophical Society and the Geographical Society of Philadelphia.

In 1925 the University of Pennsylvania conferred upon me the honorary degree of Litt.D., and in 1927 La Salle College, that of LL.D.

Without going further into details, enough data has been given, possibly too much, to show the various fields of my interests and activities.

Vacations have been spent in travel, in earlier years in Europe, more recently in this country, and a few summers in teaching, as at Columbia, University of Wisconsin, and last summer at the University of California at Berkeley.

As I look back over our undergraduate days, I am thankful that I went to Amherst College, for I cherish the happy memories of classmates and other friends, and prize the many advantages of classroom and of social life that we enjoyed.

There are, however, some changes that I would wish to make, if it were possible to take the work over again, both in my own selection of studies and in the courses offered to us. While I do not regret my classical training, I could wish that we had been given a thorough training in English composition and in modern language. I have felt the lack of such training in later years.

In these respects Amherst and other colleges have improved. My observation is, however, that the majority of students who have had a classical training, and who later on enter a graduate school, are not able to meet the requirements in modern languages for the degree of Doctor of Philosophy, namely, a sight reading knowledge of two modern foreign languages, usually French and German. This is unfortunate as these languages are necessary tools for those who desire to do advanced work in most fields. In consequence, the deficiencies must be made up while the student is engrossed in the work of his specialty. The prospective graduate student should have his attention called to these requirements sufficiently early in his college course to enable him to qualify in these languages on entering upon his graduate work.

In most of the other fields, as I review them, I regard the instruction as excellent and especially so in the classics, history, philosophy, and debating.

As a student of history I desire to pay my tribute to the memory of Professor Morse. Not only did he give us a sound and philosophical interpretation of history, but he did even more than this. He impressed upon us the importance of cultivating a judicial attitude in the study of history. In my subsequent studies, both in this country and abroad, I have never come in contact with a teacher who was so judicially minded. This was an extraordinary gift, and one from which his students must have profited.

H. V. AMES

HERMAN VANDENBURG AMES

Postscript

DR. AMES scarce lived the allotted three score years and ten. He had planned to retire at the end of the next academic year and was looking forward to a period of fruitful leisure. He had two research projects in mind, one a biography of Robert J. Walker, and the other a study of the Presidential Veto Power, but these never were to be. His memorial must be of another character.

His picture will be placed on the walls of the University. The Herman V. Ames Memorial Fund for the University Library has been started. This little book, too, will do its part. But the finest of memorials will be found in the hearts of the many who have such good reason to remember him with respect for his scholarly standards, gratitude for his guiding influence, and affection for his ever friendly interest.

www.ingramcontent.com/pod-product-compliance
Lightning Source LLC
LaVergne TN
LVHW060411220926
848484LV00015B/2408